The Power of

Natural Learning

A Simple Way to Homeschool

The Power of
Natural Learning
A Simple Way to Homeschool

Valerie Butler

The Power of Natural Learning
Published by Aspen Publishing
Santaquin, UT
www.aspenschooling.com

Copyright © 2018 by Valerie Butler
ISBN 978-0-692-13280-7

Published in the United States of America

To my extraordinary children and husband who have been with me since the beginning of all this. It was them who breathed life into the ideas of Natural Learning. They have always been, and continue to be, my inspiration, critics, proof readers, guinea pigs, supporters and cohorts. I love them dearly.

To Karie who collaborated, edited, encouraged, prompted and always maintained that this book was waiting to be born.

To the families of Aspen Academy who trusted me enough to join in the many adventures we took. I'm so grateful we were able to do it together.

Val Butler's *The Power of Natural Learning* is an excellent guide for any parent considering homeschooling, written by an expert on the subject. In fact, Val's book contains very applicable ideas for ANY parent or teacher regarding learning and child development! As a scientist and geologist, I see in the natural world amazing Environments for learning that attract interest at all ages from crawling infants all the way to seasoned professionals. Val uses these and other environments to draw out this interest naturally. Val's approach to Natural Learning focuses and builds upon the innate and individual human curiosity that drives learning throughout life. The Power of Natural Learning is a valuable resource for anyone interested in fostering and promoting learning in youth and at all stages of life!

Dr. L. Cameron Mosher: Geologist, Life Coach and author of, *I'm OK I'm Just Not Finished Yet*.

www.IWalkedOnFire.com

"Yes! This is exactly what parents are looking for!" Was my enthusiastic response when I read *Natural Learning*, by Valerie Butler. It just fit and makes so much sense I blush thinking about it. Oh how I wish I'd had this simple 3-part system for successful homeschooling years ago—lucky you! I would have had even MORE parenting fun. It almost makes me want to start a family all over again.... Read it once, then read it again with a highlighter—and get started! YOU have no excuses. These THREE *Natural Learning* principles have been time tested, kid tested and parent approved and are as easy as One, Two, Three! Come join the Happy in the World, Kid Revolution!

Karie Clingo; *Next Step* Life Coach & Author of *The Spin of Life Journal*.

Find her at KarieClingo.com

What parents are saying about —*The Power of Natural Learning*

Thank you so much for sharing your book with us. Steven and I read it together and ate it up as if it were candy. We are so excited to try all of your ideas and apply them to our family. We've made a lot of foundational principles and we're excited to start our Observations.

Steve and Cherise Cooper - Parents of 4 active children and founders of www.howtomakemoneyasakid.com

I felt like I was sitting with you and talking face to face. The chapter on Observation was excellent. I'm going to get a notebook for my class and my son and start noticing more. There is something about writing it down that is crucial to the thinking process. I thought the examples were interesting and inspiring. I loved the example you gave from your own journals. I wanted more of those. I think this book is wonderful! I didn't want it to end.

Natashia Wulfenstein - Mother of 4, Director of Aspen Cooperative

The philosophies in this book will TRANSFORM your homeschool! By implementing the simple and effective tools Valerie teaches, you will become the mentor your children need to achieve their highest potential. You will better understand how to make learning enjoyable and engaging for your whole family. I'm thrilled with how much my own children are learning using the principles in this book!

Brittney Moon - Attorney & homeschooling mom of 3 boys

"Natural learning sends the message to our kids that we honor them, accept them, and care about them. I love that Valerie is so able to explain the nitty gritty and comfort a mother's heart as she explains how simple, effective and doable this approach is. "

Machiel Pulley - Homeschool mother of 7

Table of Contents

Introduction

There has never been a better and more crucial time to homeschool your children. While there are many difficulties facing us right now, we also live in a time of abundant opportunity with the potential for many rich experiences and blessings. By teaching our families at home we can forge an environment where our children can confidently explore, learn and be strengthened by you, while preparing for their amazing futures.

I must say that learning with children at home is an impressive and bold undertaking. It quite literally takes blood, sweat and tears. Every single day is a new adventure and some are more delightful than others.

Whether you are just starting your homeschool, deciding whether to homeschool, or are an expert homeschooler, you are in the process of demanding and fulfilling times. I hope to meet you face to face someday and listen as you tell me *your* story of homeschooling. This is *my* story, and after almost 20 years of researching, experimenting and discovering I'm thrilled to share it with you. Thank you for the privilege.

This book will give you a peek into my transformation from a traditional public school mom to a homeschool mentor and everything in between. I took my own children from public school to homeschool, from private school to whatever worked best for them. Yes, it was a wild ride and undeniably magnificent! I made some mistakes along the way that you can avoid as you grow your homeschool into that powerful environment you've envisioned.

I'm excited to share the tools I've discovered for building a lively learning environment while saving you time, money and frustration. I want you and your family to wake up in the morning so full of excitement for learning that you jump in your van only to realize you are still wearing your pajamas!

Through these pages I know you will receive the confidence to see your children's educational journey through with an unwavering faith that you can absolutely do it.

1
First Things First

My husband just finished pouring cement in our backyard. It took him only a few hours to pour it, but the preparation leading up to the pour took him weeks. He had to dig out several inches of grass and dirt, level it, bring in gravel for drainage purposes, level it again...you get the picture. Because of his preparation the cement looks amazing and he is very proud of it. His foundation was strong and sure.

Your homeschool foundation must be strong and sure as well. Why have you chosen to homeschool your children? There is a reason you are doing what you do. There is a reason you want your children to learn specific things. Do you know what those reasons are? If you are going to succeed, when big and little challenges come, you must get very clear on the answers to these questions. You must have a rock-solid foundation.

Once you dig deep enough and prepare your foundation, you can build your homeschool with confidence. On days when you are convinced the whole thing was a bad idea and you're ready to throw in the towel, you can come back to your family's foundational principles and be reassured that you are absolutely doing the right thing. Together let's walk through the process of determining your family's foundational principles.

Begin by listing ten things that you feel are important for your children to learn. This is a rewarding activity and will take some careful thought, however as you take the time to genuinely consider what teachings you value for your family, you will reap great benefits in the coming weeks and months. It might mean digging through the drawers to find a notebook and pen, but please stop and do it now!

With your list in front of you, you're ready to work through the process of finding the motivating principles behind your decision to homeschool. This process will include several questions - always with the word "why" included. Keep asking yourself "why" until you are sure that you have found the core reason. These core reasons will be the principles you will build on.

Perhaps one thing on your list is **reading.** You want your children to learn to read. That's reasonable. WHY? Why do you want your children to learn to read?

You might say, "I want them to read because it opens the door to knowledge."

I would ask you, "Why is it important that they gain knowledge?"

You might say, "Because knowledge will ensure their success in college and in a career."

Me: "Why is this important to you?"

You: "Because then they can be happy, have a good job and support a family."

Me: "And why would it be important for them to be happy and support their family?"

You: "Because they will feel good about being productive and working hard."

Me: "Why is this important?"

You: "So that they can realize their potential and find talents to develop and share."

Me: "Why is this important?"

You: "It will allow them to serve their family, their community and be a good example to others."

Me: "The reason you want your children to learn to read is so that they will eventually serve and be a good example to others?

You: "Yes."

Obviously this is a hypothetical conversation and your dialog will look different. The important point is to get to the nitty gritty of "why." It works well to have this conversation with your spouse. First have your spouse answer the questions as you ask them, then turn it around and have your spouse ask the questions of you. Record each of the conversations. If your spouse isn't available, invite a trusted friend or family member to help — someone who knows your family well.

Let's walk through one more example. You might want your children to **learn to be honest**. Why?

You: "So that they can understand integrity."

Me: "Why is this important?"

You: "So that people can count on them and they can experience peace that comes through honesty."

Me: "Why would this be important?"

You: "Because then they can be an example of goodness and can have a clear conscience."

Me: "And why is this so valuable?"

You: "It contributes to the goodness in the world."

Me: "And why is it important to do this?"

You: "Because it honors God and shows gratitude to Him."

Me: "So the reason you want your children to learn to be honest is to honor God and show gratitude to Him?"

You: "Yes."

So far, in this theoretical conversation, your family's foundational principles for learning would be:

- To give service and be a good example to others

- To honor God and show gratitude to Him

This is the beginning of an impressive list. Of course this will look different for each family, but through this process you will construct a foundation that will boost you up and give you strength to persist. Post your list somewhere that you will see it frequently. Repeat it to yourself often. On mornings when the house is a mess, there is no milk in the fridge and your five-year-old woke up on the wrong side of the bed for the third time in 3 days, you will look at your foundational principles, take a deep breath and smile. You are doing great things!

Again, if you read through these examples without DOING the process for yourself, ACTION is now necessary. Please take those few minutes and get it done. You'll be very grateful that you did.

On to my story...

2

My Story and the Three Minute Conversation

The countdown had begun! I was months away from living a life I had previously only imagined. I was a mom of five kids living in Louisville, Kentucky, and my youngest child was about to enter kindergarten. For years I had dreamt about this day because it meant I would have an entire 6 hours a day—Monday through Friday—with a house all to myself! No whining kids, no unexpected messes, no interruptions! I gleefully thought of all the things I would accomplish without the many distractions. There was nothing, or so I thought, that could entice me to give that up. Then came the three-minute conversation. The conversation that would change all of my carefully laid plans. That moment in time went something like this...

The front door flew open as my daughter announced she was home from school. My son followed slowly behind with his Pokémon backpack dragging on the wood floor. He plopped down in the nearest chair and put his head in his hands. It was a clear indicator that this particular school day was not going down as a "top ten greatest." I asked him what was wrong, as any decent, caring mother should, and he shrugged his shoulders as any upset little boy would.

"Come on, Bud," I coaxed, "Did something happen at school today?"
Tears came first and then the story...

"I had my head on my desk cause I was kind of tired, (sob) and my teacher made me stand up at the side of the table, (sob) without a chair, for a really long time, (sob, sob)."

"How long?" I questioned as I felt little prickles mounting inside me.

"A long time," He surmised.

Prior to this moment I had certainly had those difficult conversations with myself regarding our children and their "education." My eleven-year-old daughter had been teased relentlessly by some of the boys in her class because of her early maturation. For several years my husband and I had watched as liberal social programs, that we were uncomfortable with, were becoming more and more a required part of public education. At the same time it seemed that prayer, God and even patriotism were diminishing.

Evenings were often spent with sheets of homework that made all of us grumpy and took away precious family time. All of this was in the back of my mind, but what were my options? Homeschooling sounded so daunting and I kept pushing it aside.

It might have been the sunshine, the chocolate I had just devoured or the planets in alignment that day, but my son's tear-stained face gave me the courage to make the tough but crucial decision I had been avoiding. I was going to bring my children home for good.

I suppose I should be grateful to my son's teacher for that final push in helping me make such a grandiose decision, but at the time I was not so generous with my thoughts.

I still remember walking the long, dimly-lit hallway of the elementary school trying to find the office. I was woefully inexperienced in asserting myself and wasn't sure of the procedure to remove my three youngest children from school. There were four or five women in the office as I hesitantly stepped through the door.

"May I help you?" one of them asked.

"I would like to pull my children out of school?" (I'm quite sure I posed it as a question.)

The first lady looked to one of the others who must have been in charge.

"May I ask *why* you want to pull your children out of school?" she questioned.

"I have decided to homeschool," was my astounding reply.

Dead silence.

"Is there a form I need to fill out?" That's all I could think of to end the awkward silence.

Then she stated, "You know it's very difficult to teach children. Are you sure you want to do this?"

Of course I wasn't sure. In fact I was in complete panic mode and probably not far from tears. That's when my fighting spirit rose to the surface as I thought of that three minute conversation with my six-year-old son. Despite my fear and uncertainties, I somehow managed to jot down the personal information of all three of my elementary school children, filled out the form and left. I'm not sure what those nice ladies were thinking, probably something like, "You poor thing," but I never looked back to see.

It didn't take long for the terror to set in. Although I knew I had done the right thing, I had no clue where to turn next. I was now officially committed to the single craziest thing a mother could do — educate her children at home. At this time there was no Google, no Siri, and I didn't know any other homeschoolers in the area. I was in desperate need of information and a stalwart support system.

The next morning I called a good friend who lived in Utah. She also happened to be the "world's greatest homeschooling mom."

"But I don't even know the names of the Greek gods!" I awkwardly admitted to her, as I felt the wave of frustration rising in me.

I have to confess that I secretly thought my friend was a wee bit crazy for choosing to keep her four children at home...now I just wanted her decade of experience and wisdom poured into my head within the hour. While that wasn't possible, my friend did leave me with a cherished gift of confidence. She talked with me, answered a myriad of questions, and assured me it would all be just fine.

And so began *my* personal path of learning. I've never read as voraciously as I did in preparation for this huge undertaking. I've never asked so many questions. I pondered over it, prayed over it, lost sleep over it and eventually watched over the learning of my amazing children. I realize now the greatest thing about homeschooling has been the adventure of figuring it out together—every exhilarating, exhausting, memorable moment of it!

My years of learning, praying, and reading led to some monumental discoveries about education; little secrets that have produced amazing outcomes. In the next chapter I'll share the most important one with you. I like to call it the "The Secret of the Century."

3
The Secret of the Century

This one secret will unlock excitement and wonder in your children's learning. It will decrease planning and prep time, not to mention save you countless hours of tears and frustration later on. My own discovery of this principle has come through hours of studying, experimenting, practicing and implementing, though it should have been clear years ago.

What is this Secret of the Century? Listen carefully... then listen again and then write it down for posterity. It is sure to be your next refrigerator magnet or vinyl lettering over the kitchen door. Here it is:

Learning is what we do. I repeat **LEARNING IS WHAT WE DO!**

It is the very essence of life and the purpose for being. It is how God made us. It stands to reason that we are born with the ability to do so. There are other names for this, but I like to call it "Natural Learning" which simply means, "Let your child learn." Let them learn what is important to them. Let them learn and foster *their* talents! Let *them* take *you* by the hand and pull you along as they discover the newness that surrounds them.

Natural Learning is letting your child learn from their mistakes and your example, learning to have confidence in their ability to make decisions, letting them learn to trust their gut. It requires trust from you. It doesn't come with a simple checklist or set of manuals to follow. Rather it suggests that your family write the manual as you go. Each chapter will be as different as the child who is creating it.

Young children are experts at Natural Learning. They love to learn about almost anything. Just watch them! They can pull a stool up to the sink, fill it with soap and water and be engaged indefinitely. In their hands, a stick transforms to a

20

sword, a pistol or a magic wand. They can turn a drive through the canyon into an adventure brimming with pirates and hideouts and treasures, "Argh."

When my kids were small they would go into the garage and pull out the cooler; the one with the blue bottom and the white top that everyone takes camping. Next they would turn on the hose, fill it to the brim with water and go "swimming." They figured this out because they wanted a swimming pool. Nobody had to teach them, they just did it. There wasn't a classroom, a desk or a lesson plan. If there had been, I'm sure the joy of making the swimming pool would have lost its charm. Somebody might have told them that it wasn't a very *big* swimming pool, or that it didn't contain the proper chemicals or that they weren't, in fact, swimming but merely sitting in a cooler of water. However, they didn't care about all of that. They played and splashed and made up games and had a marvelous time. That's Natural Learning.

One young man, whose family I mentored, had an amazing ability to build anything out of Legos. His mother had asked him to finish his writing homework which consisted of a five-page paper. He was not the least bit interested and had been putting it off for days. She took some advice from me and asked her son what *he* would like to write about if he could choose the topic. He told her he would write about castles and knights and armor and courageous battles. She encouraged him to build his castle from Legos and then tell her the story that went along with it. He built the castle and the words started to flow. *Twenty-four* pages later she became concerned that he would never be able to type this exciting story since he was not yet proficient in keyboard skills. She volunteered to type the pages that exceeded his original five-page assignment.

He replied by saying, "No Mom. If you type it then it won't be *my* story!"

That evening he finished typing the entire 24 pages by himself. What changed? The assignment was still expected, but now it was his project. He got caught up in *his* imaginings and *his* creations — the story was simply a by-product of his adventure. That's Natural Learning!

After I brought my kids home from public school, I felt excited and I also felt lost. I knew I didn't want to just mimic the worksheets and textbooks that were shoved so tightly in their backpacks, yet I felt compelled to make sure they were at least as "smart" as the rest of the kids on the block. We started by copying the only system I was familiar with. It hadn't occurred to me that children can learn without a formal classroom and teacher. I had somehow tied learning to a few mandatory things: reading, writing, math, science and social studies. So I bought each child a little journal, to encourage writing, along with a math workbook.

Quickly, I found myself frustrated when they didn't get their work done and when my preschooler didn't seem to grasp the idea of phonics. I watched as the pile of dirty clothes got higher, tried to ignore the telephone and felt guilty when I couldn't get to all of my oldest daughter's high school activities. And then, we decided to open a bookstore with a good friend of ours! I know that sounds like the last thing I needed to add to our hectic life, but in reality it was exactly what I needed at the time to teach me the wonderful art of Natural Learning.

While working to open the bookstore we scrapped most of the *bookwork* and started shopping for *bookshelves*. We made phone calls to book suppliers and to local authors. We had book signings and story time. The kids took turns coming to work with me. We were so busy we really didn't have time for "school" but we learned like we had never learned before! When the kids didn't go to work with me they would plan their own activities at home—with a little supervision—or we would plan an excursion together.

I watched as my children's **wonder came to life**. It became clear to me that children like to **discover**, **explore** and **create** all by themselves—as long as mom is close by to "come see." Whenever I heard the words, "Hey I know, let's...." I was sure that something amazing was about to happen.

I *finally* realized that my children had an incredible desire to learn about any number of things, and that's when we started to have fun. We spent a lot of time at the Science Museum. We discovered a Shaker Village just sixty minutes from our home. We visited the beautiful ranches of Lexington and the Louisville Slugger manufacturing plant. We found Huber Farms, Zany Brany (our neighborhood toy store), basketball games and lots of parks to explore. When it rained we ran outside to play in it. In the fall there were so many leaves that a small 3-year-old could get lost for the day. We discovered fossil beds in Ohio, new trails to forge, and amazing historical sights. Everywhere we looked there was something we had never seen before. That is how life is for our young children. Every day is full of first-time experiences and that alone is thrilling.

Natural Learning makes for a beautiful life as we step back and allow our children to learn through their own explorations and curiosity. I've learned that life is a wise, nurturing, sometimes exacting teacher—the very best there is. We are her humble assistants. Together delightful things happen.

Natural Learning does not suggest that children need no guidance. Children need much guidance, but they need it in a way that accounts for their unique talents and interests. At the end of the day, learning looks completely different for each of us. As you implement Natural Learning in your homeschool, your children will thrive in their educational journey. You will lead them more effectively because you understand their interests, talents, and personalities. Once you understand their needs and talents, you can offer heartfelt suggestions to open their eyes to new ideas. Because your experiences are much broader than your child's, you have an opportunity to provide a huge variety of ideas for them to explore. Many influential men and women have excelled because of the teaching they received from passionate parents and mentors.

Watch your children become independent and strong when given time to explore what they are most excited about. Our next topic will launch the Natural Learning process.

4
Observation

Think of Natural Learning as the secret to ultimate homeschooling. However, in order to utilize this secret you must understand the first and most important step in Natural Learning: **Observation.** If you are willing to master the art of Observation and implement its power, you will be successful in Natural Learning. Observation is simple, and because of its simplicity our inclination is to stop doing it after only a brief time. However, the philosophy of Natural Learning is unlocked through patient Observation.

A story from the life of renowned naturalist William Hamilton Gibson in his book *Eye Spy* illustrates the power of Observation and how it shaped who he became.

"I was very young, and playing in the woods. I tossed over the fallen leaves, when I came across a chrysalis. There was nothing remarkable in that, for I knew what it was. But, as I held the object in my hand a butterfly slowly emerged, then fluttered in my fingers. Suddenly the spiritual view of a new, or of another life struck me. I saw in this jewel, born from an unadorned casket, some inkling of immortality. Yes, that butterfly breaking from its chrysalis in my hand shaped my future career."

Observation is a tool used by the most influential men and women from history. Thomas Edison used Observation to discover the filament that would finally unlock the power of electricity. As the Wright brothers observed soaring birds, they noticed that birds change the shape of their wings as they glide. This led them to create an ingenious technique called "wing warping". Leonardo DaVinci was a master observer and recorded thousands of pages of observations in his famous notebooks. Observation will help *you* to unlock the power of learning in your homeschool.

Observation opens our eyes and allows us to see our children in a new light. As we use the power of Observation we watch our kids emerge from their own personal chrysalis and take flight. Observation allows the privilege of curious exploration in any number of settings. The goal is to watch them without expectations and without schedules. Just sit and observe!

Observation begins with a pen and a notebook. Your Observation Notebook is very important and will be unique to you. It will be a place for your notes and insights. It is a place for you to write, draw and record each day of adventure. Here are a few ideas that will make your Observation time count:

First: Use the same notebook every time. Buy one that costs a little more than your other notebooks. We're all guilty of buying a new notebook, to keep track of any number of things, only to find that a week later we can't remember where we left it. Your Observation Notebook needs to become almost an extension of your hand! It cannot be left on the coffee table where it might fall prey to the toddler with a handful of crayons. Don't leave it in the van to be kicked under the seat. It should be protected and safeguarded. If done right you will find yourself growing very attached to your Observation Notebook and its valuable research. It will become like a dear friend to you. Take care of your friend!

Second: Be honest in your Observations. This is for you to look at, not for your social media friends to scrutinize. If you notice that your six- year-old seems to find joy in pushing others down, write about it. You can address the concern later, but put it all in your Observation Notebook.

Third: For organizational purposes, have a different section in your notebook for each child. It is also helpful to specify a "summary spot" somewhere at the bottom of the page. Here you can note what stood out to you - along with little inspirations that come to you.

Fourth: Use highlighting pens when something really stands out to you. While I was observing the moms in my study group, I would highlight in red the thoughts that I considered particularly important at the time. This way it was easier to find things when I was reviewing.

Fifth: While observing, vary your days and your activities. This will give you a better view of your child. Children behave differently at museums than they do at gymnasiums. Plan to attend concerts and organize picnics. It's critical that you observe your kids in their home environment as well as in brand new settings.

Keep your Observation Notebook close by throughout your day and jot down ideas as they come to you. I would recommend that you consciously set aside an hour each day to start yourself on the journey of observing and recording. Add more time as the weeks move on. Strive to do this religiously for two or three months. Soon it will become a refreshing habit. Many moms do Observation for one or two days and think it is sufficient. This is simply not enough time. To see your child through new eyes and to get past your prior assumptions about them, you have to give yourself several weeks of Observation.

As you learn to master the skill of Observation you will find yourself getting excited about future plans with your children. Watch for patterns to emerge. Little inspirations and insights will come into your mind.

Mothers whom I have mentored will often say,

"But I already know my children. I know how they will react to any given situation."

We all think that we know our children, and certainly we do, however, sometimes we know them as WE want them to be, not necessarily as THEY really are. Weeks of Observation will help us to see patterns and subtleties that we may have overlooked. Observation opens a series of questions. How do your children interact with others—with you? What favorite activities do they choose to participate in? Do they like to spend time alone? If so, what do they engage in over and over? Are they always by your side? Do they prefer to play with others?

What habits are they picking up? Are they comfortable giving their opinion? Are they far too opinionated? What places do they like to visit and why? If allowed to do anything, what occupies their time?

Here are samples of my own Observations with our study group:

> "The ceramic shop was a hit and every child was engaged the entire time. Moms were also very engaged. It took Taylor almost an hour to decide on the item he wanted to paint. Noelle picked her project out immediately. All of the children, from two to fourteen, asked if they could come back again. I learned that we all like to create something of our own, that there is excitement in learning a new process and then doing it."

> "The kids loved the potter's wheel and waited in line for quite a while to have a turn. The Pulley family also took time to make their own incubator which Deb helped with. The Anderson's had already made one and showed it to everyone—along with the eggs they had inside. It will be fun to see how many eggs hatch.
>
> After our activities we talked about how we will choose to finish our last three weeks together.
>
> Marianne talked to me about how she is letting her kids continue to choose what they would like to do

but is limiting Braman's video games. She said her mother bought Braman a math book and he really turned up his nose. He does love mind math and after one week of talking about "squared" numbers he asked his mom what that meant. Now he understands and loves to give the answers.

Marianne also asked about Environments and said she was thinking that she would take her Observations of her children and what they have shown an interest in, write them on little slips of paper and put them in a jar for the kids to pull out. This would then become their activities for the day. I told her it was a great idea and that I would like to borrow it and put it on my blog! *Remember to ask her to share it with the other parents." (Originally Highlighted in red so I could find this reference quickly)

Observation is that simple. Just write about what you see.

Add some personal notes to help you remember little ideas that come. Ask yourself—"What do the children like to talk about? What natural strengths are they developing? What traits are they cultivating? What talents are emerging? Finally, what are you learning as you watch them explore?"

Machiel, one of the moms in our study group, used the power of Observation to open her eyes to some challenging realizations. She generously shared these thoughts with me.

"I had a breakthrough this week as I was observing my children. I even drew a little light bulb next to my words as I recorded them in my Observation Notebook. I noticed that my children often looked to me for permission to say what they thought I wanted to hear, instead of what they really wanted to say. I realized there have been a lot of positive things happening because of Natural Learning. My kids have accomplished things that they wouldn't have done before. Noelle has planned parties and written invitations and made agendas. We've had a lot of sewing going on. We had a serger that literally sat in the box for 6 months...now that we've been doing Natural Learning Cherish has been searching on YouTube and she's learned how to thread it and she's making things — measuring fabric...she made a nightgown for her sister. She largely did it without my help. We've had a lot of neat things happen like that. It's been interesting to see them make a list of the things they're interested in. When I asked, 'What do you care about, what matters to you?' Some of those things have surprised me. I need to give them more freedom to choose and make their own decisions and express their opinions.

I'm learning more and more that God gave us our agency and then the first thing we do is try to take it away from our kids. At the end of the day, if I was the one that dictated the learning, if I was the one that told the kids what to do and they did it, I would feel a sense of accomplishment because we covered these things. It was truly about my feelings and it's been hard sometimes to let go of that and let them take the lead."

Observation helps you see things in a new light; not just about your children but about yourself as well. Observation allows you to see more clearly the budding interests unique to each individual. When nurtured with opportunity, love, and encouragement these interests often blossom into talents. You will be inspired to guide your children as you quietly watch them and then record your thoughts. A "personal curriculum" of sorts will emerge for each child and will become a resource that you will add to frequently and return to often. You will continue to practice and modify until the art of Observation becomes second nature.

Why so much emphasis on Observation? Because it assures a strong foundation. Through Observation you discover the heart of your children and what makes them tick. You and your children are now prepared to design the perfect learning Environments. Let's get started.

Note on Media and Observation

My husband programs computers and he is really good at it. I am so grateful for his talent and the bountiful way it has provided for our family. Many future careers will be tied to electronics—more and more are popping up every day. Certainly we need to give our children the opportunity to explore this medium as we see fit and as they are mature enough to understand. Having said that, I don't recommend "screens" be a part of Observation. How long to allow your children to be on electronic devices is a personal decision, but it is difficult to observe your child while they are being entertained by the computer the television or the iPad. The only thing to observe is generally a blank stare.

5
Environments

Now that you understand the skill of Observation you will most likely find your mind drifting toward many future plans with your children. You've spent the past several weeks watching and listening and writing. You are ready for step Two: **Designing Environments.** This step is my favorite part of Natural Learning. All of your preparation and dedication will pay off as you visit with your children about future activities, projects, explorations and discoveries.

Your Observations should have refined your impressions. You are ready to boldly and powerfully take on the creation of

Environments. **Environments will take the place of curriculum**. Environments enhance the individual and fit their personal strengths and curiosity. An Environment is something inviting, attractive and exhilarating. It should help your child feel that they are in their element and should be accompanied by eagerness and anticipation. Whereas the success of a curriculum is measured with A's, B's and C's, Environments are measured with "oohs, aahs and wows!"

Let go of the vision you have of every little body seated around the dining room table with eager, happy faces just waiting for you to speak so they can obey. It's quite possible this will never be. How about a new idea—something infinitely better—you get to take your classroom anywhere you choose, anywhere your children choose and anywhere their curious little minds can conceive! See yourself wading through the river, grocery shopping with your child as they search for all the necessary ingredients to make dinner, fabric stores, pet stores, homeless shelters—not to live in, but to serve at—libraries, concerts, street fairs, farmer's markets, thrift stores, plays, airports, planetariums... to name a few. You and your children will have the time of your lives in this new undertaking.

Your Observation Notebook becomes your blueprint for setting up Environments. As you read through your notes let your own imagination expand and see the world through the eyes of your child.

Perhaps through your expert Observation you discovered that one child loves to be outside getting dirty while collecting sticks, rocks and creepy crawlies. Maybe you have a child who engages in questions—about everything—or does music inspire them? Do they like to run and climb, or were they more interested in observing a dandelion or a ladybug? Do you have a daredevil on your hands or one who is more reserved and hesitant? You may have a child who loves to cook, one who loves to build, one who loves to draw and one who doesn't seem to love anything—in this case be patient and give them more time to figure things out. Your Observation Notebook will ignite ideas for future Environments.

Just suppose with me that you found a "budding astronomer" in your family. Ask yourself, "What might an

Environment look like for an astronaut in training?" Most definitely a telescope—a map of the night sky, as well as glow-in-the-dark stars and planets to place strategically on bedroom walls and ceilings. (One of my daughters did this years ago and they are still there. Even today my adult children enjoy turning out the lights in her bedroom and watching the stars come out!) Your future astronaut will need lots of books about planets, stars and black holes, time with Mom and Dad to plan some star gazing opportunities at the local planetarium, attendance at an astronomy club, a subscription to astronomy magazines, NASA's website and so forth. You are just trying to get the ball rolling from your Observations and then watch your child take off.

How about a child who loves to dabble with paintbrushes and all things messy? They will flourish with a sketchbook and a drawer full of water colors, pastels, clay, acrylics and charcoal. Also helpful will be aprons, an old table or desk, rags and a perfect place to display their beautiful, and not so beautiful, creations. They will cherish their trips to the library to peruse books, as well as field trips to local museums and street fairs. Some fun tutorials on the internet will assist them as they mature in their interest. Art classes in their chosen subject of interest comes later and an adult mentor is invaluable to boost confidence and knowledge. You can watch them joyfully spend hours creating their next masterpiece.

I promised you that Natural Learning would help save money, yet some Environments can appear costly. Set your budget, then spend time together at flea markets, thrift stores, yard sales and the "free" section of your local classified ads. I get most of my resource books from library sales and used bookstores. Some of my favorite memories are mapping out the best yard sales in surrounding towns and getting up early with my children to go "treasure hunting." Of course we left the babies home with dad so we could find the perfect items without frustration. Acquiring the needed materials for Environments turns into fun family outings. It also allows children to learn to be frugal as they break open their own piggy banks to purchase some of the needed supplies.

Environments should be as different as your family's interests. As an example, two of my daughters had a love for horses. It almost drove me crazy! I finally found a friend in our neighborhood who was willing to take them to the farm where she stabled her horses. My girls would clean tack for her in exchange for riding lessons. Brenda had a way with horses and she had a way with children. I was never able to get them to work as hard as they did for her. Eventually she took us to one of her horse shows, where we all saw firsthand what professional horse riding can look like. It was an amazing opportunity. In this case, the Environment consisted of a willing mentor, her knowledge and resources—including a horse—HALLELUJAH!— my willingness to drive them to the stables each week and their commitment to clean tack in order to pay for their lessons. They loved this Environment. They were eager and determined and they worked their little tails off. I didn't have to say a word.

An added benefit was when Brenda invited my kids to come over once a week for some really remarkable art activities. They looked forward to it because they were creating something unique and original. I looked forward to it because I got to spend an hour at the gym!

My son, on the other hand, became very interested in Pokémon cards. He wanted to buy them, trade them, read them and battle with them. We found a local bookstore that had "Pokémon Night" where children could come together and do all of their "Pokémon stuff" - stuff I still don't quite understand. Kyle loved it. From this he taught himself to read. I don't even remember helping him much. There were times he would ask me how to pronounce a particular word and then somehow he just figured it out. Here the Environment was simply finding others with a common Pokémon interest. We also organized ways for Kyle to earn money for his habitual Pokémon card purchases. His Dad and I took turns taking him to the weekly gatherings and supervising all of the fun. Kyle thrived in his Environment.

I quickly realized that the kids were learning their basic math, reading, science, etc. without workbooks, textbooks or lesson plans. What a great relief!

The critical factor for Environments is planning them according to your Observations and the children's input. I remember enrolling Kyle in flag football because boys are supposed to like football right? He didn't like this Environment at all; in fact it brought him great misery. Had I understood the concept of Observation at this time I might have noted that he wasn't aggressive or competitive, and we could have avoided the whole miserable thing. I chalk it up to a good learning experience.

Outdoor Environments are favorites with most children. Nature brings out the very best in us. We can climb trees, put our toes in the sand, jump rope, count dandelions, share a picnic, wade in the pond, make mud pies, watch bees gather pollen, build a lemonade stand as well as write in our journals and do a math lesson. Everything is better in the sunshine!

Environments can reach to include a concert, a basketball game, service for a friend, climbing a tree, a day spent with Grandma, a Lego table, a game of hopscotch or flying kites. Our children will learn something meaningful from every one of these experiences. Let me share an example of a recent Environment I enjoyed with our study group:

"The days were just warming to 50 degrees from a long winter. We grabbed our backpacks, water bottles and stroller and headed for the river trail close to home.

The kids found a tree with a branch hanging over the bank of the river so we stopped to climb. We stayed until everyone got their fill of "not falling" out of the tree. A little further down the trail we decided we were hungry and got out our lunches. We had brought along some flint and steel after mentioning the book, "My Side of the Mountain" earlier that morning. The sparks were flying, but we couldn't get a flame. Though the younger kids lost interest, the older kids were determined. We learned it is very difficult to start a fire without matches but resolved that we would keep practicing. We threw some rocks in the river and found it was not a great place to skip a rock because of the height of the bank. We ate our sandwiches and talked– about everything! Slowly we made our way back to the car in time to get the little ones home for a nap. I still smile as I remember that day."

Remember, often an Environment will foster an interest in a child that will stay for a time and then be gone. Not everything your child starts will be finished or mastered, but it will give experience and memories. Give your children the chance to "try" things without feeling guilty if they don't love them as much as they thought they would. With encouragement they will find what it is that really drives them. When we couple a child's wonder with a parent's reassurance, learning is the natural outcome—learning that connects to the heart of the child.

Perhaps the most critical Environments are those that you organize to teach your children life's lessons. In Great Britain a study was done which included a survey of over 2000 parents. When asked what they felt was most important to teach their children, saying "please" and "thank you" was number one. What is number one for your family? The list from Great Britain included 59 things. Some were as simple as tying shoes or riding a bike. I've included the entire list in Appendix 2. What would you consider your top 20?

Many, if not all, of the moms I have mentored feel that it is important to have a clean house—not a spotless house, but an organized house. This makes for a more pleasant experience when learning together. Keeping a clean house becomes an Environment—one that Mom depends on and kids learn greatly from. Folding clothes can happen while mom is reading a cherished book out loud. Even a three-year-old can take their clothes to the bedroom and put them in a dresser drawer with a little bit of help. Meal preparation is another fabulous Environment when the family chooses to take it on together. Yes, the kitchen will be a bit of a disaster afterward, but cleaning up together is another important Environment. It is much more fun when we do it together and is an important teaching time.

Other life-skill Environments may be learning to change a spark plug on the lawn mower, or the oil in the car. My 25-year-old daughter was determined to change her own oil and found a friend who gave her some lessons. Her father, and "yours truly," are fond of *Jiffy Lube*. She now can do it herself and is very proud of that fact.

Discussions about money—how to save it, when to spend it, and how to invest it, all serve as important Environments. I remember teaching a class on finances to some older children who had never had the experience of setting up a bank account. We made an appointment with the local credit union and got approval from their parents to open a savings account for each of them. They loved the idea of having their own bank account. It put them in the adult world and gave them personal responsibility over their money. Taking time to talk about saving, spending and investing can become an exhilarating Environment. The list goes on, but remember that Environments are inclusive of all of those things that foster your children's curiosity and instill in them your family's foundational principles.

A Word to the Wise: Before jumping into Environments with older children (approximately age 8 and up), plan some time together. Two on one is best—just Mom and Dad and the child. Make this a very important time by taking them to lunch or dinner. Share with them the things you have been observing. Show them your Observation Notebook and ask them how they feel about it. Ask them about their likes and dislikes. What is on their list of activities and interests?

Work together to map out Environments for the coming weeks and listen carefully to their input, writing it down in your Observation Notebook. Let them know that their opinion is important to you and they will respond with excitement. As children grow it is extremely critical to plan together and to let them take the lead with their learning. This will be especially important as they reach their teenage years and are ready to make bigger plans. They will be prepared to set important goals regarding college, internships, career choices, service opportunities, etc., because of the freedom they have been given in their own learning. Natural Learning develops our children's ability to think for themselves and to solve problems on their own.

For younger children, your enthusiastic suggestions and assistance will be needed. Help get them started with a few fun Environments and they will take it from there.

6
Swinging for the Fence with Excursions

Once in a while I highly recommend that you swing big and aim for the fence! Plan something extraordinary with your family! Eight years ago we took some time to study the history of the Renaissance. I keep a small "bucket list" of sorts tucked away in my closet and at the top of my list was a trip to Italy. For some reason I am fascinated with the likes of DaVinci, Michelangelo, Raphael, the Roman Forum, the Coliseum, vineyards and the whole romantic idea of Italy!

I realized this was the perfect time to combine my own captivation of Italy with our history studies and plan a trip to Europe. I presented this monumental plan to my own family and a few other friends. We ended up with a group of 20 committed individuals and eagerly laid out plans to travel to Italy, Greece, Jerusalem, Croatia and Turkey. It certainly wasn't without its challenges, but every step of our planning was thrilling. The trip itself was truly life changing! Though words will never completely describe our trip, let me attempt to share a few thoughts I recorded shortly after we returned home:

> "Standing in front of the Last Supper and Michelangelo's Pieta was a magnificent and spiritual experience. Tears came naturally and for a moment I felt the sacrifice and passion that went into these masterpieces. I **thought to myself, "How does one reach the point of creating something that invokes such emotion as I was feeling?"** I didn't have the answer, but I desperately wanted to understand. I wanted to find that inspiration for my own life. I wanted to create something that could move another person to tears.
>
> The answer came later as I read this thought. "The more you trust and rely upon the Spirit, the greater your capacity to create." That was the answer. Such a simple thought but how true. As we rely upon the Spirit to direct us, God's light will open our minds and increase our talents so that we may have the capacity to create a masterpiece – as did DaVinci. It takes practice and our first attempts may seem childish and unsophisticated, but as we persist we will experience success."

Now, years later, our children and the many friends who went with us, still talk about our trip with awe. So many extraordinary memories are in my heart where they continue to invoke gratitude and joy. I will be forever grateful that we made the sacrifices to plan and prepare and experience this astounding adventure!

Another "swing for the fence" moment happened as we made the decision to travel to Monterey, Mexico for humanitarian service. This idea came because I wanted to help my teenage students get beyond themselves, to serve and to see past their myopic views of the world. Teenagers are transitioning into adulthood as they hit Jr. High and High School. Sometimes they just don't know what to do with the whole process; we've all been through it and it is anything but easy. As a mentor of teenagers, I had the desire to get my students serving others in a very powerful way and to feel the nobility that comes from it. I wanted them as far away from a classroom as we could get. I wanted it to be a real and emotional experience.

I still remember presenting the plan. At first parents and students were speechless. Who could blame them? I was still stunned myself. Slowly I saw their eyes open up and the possibilities of the opportunity emerge. There was enthusiasm and ideas and dreams beginning to take shape.

Next came a taste of reality as we mapped out our financial road to Mexico. We explored many different kinds of fundraisers. We made and sold pizzas, held carwashes, sold personal belongings - one young man even sold his bed! We solicited local businesses, held yard sales and hosted a food booth at our annual city celebration. This turned out to be a complete flop! We each earned a whopping $10, but we began to learn what was and what was not productive and that was valuable information.

Finally, with a lot of hard work we had the money we needed. In the meantime we learned about the process of applying for passports, attempting to learn a foreign language, booking airplane tickets and so much more.

We have taken five different expeditions to Mexico where we have served families, schools, and orphanages. We mixed cement, built a cinderblock home, shared talents, made new friends, and went shopping with pesos instead of dollars. We learned to communicate in our broken Spanish. Above all, we

56

have been blessed to see the culture and meet the beautiful people of Mexico. The lessons taught while on these trips far surpass anything that could be created in a classroom setting. It is Natural Learning on a very high level. Yes it is difficult and rare, but worth every sacrifice.

I have also known families who have trained together for 5K runs, learned to scuba dive, built a log cabin by hand and started a family business. Whatever the "fence" looks like for your family, sit the whole team down and talk about it, then put some power behind that bat and make it happen!

By utilizing Observation, Environments and Excursions, your family will be able to incorporate Natural Learning simply and effectively. There is still **one magical resource to talk about that is absolutely critical to Natural Learning...Stories!**

Note: Our Mexico experiences were so powerful that I am teaming up with FFHE, the group that organized our trips. Each time someone purchases one of my books, a portion of the proceeds will go directly to FFHE to help the children in Mexico. Take time today to visit their website at www.ffhe.info and get involved in some way. It is a perfect Environment to teach your children about service. You and your family will soon feel the blessings of sharing with those who need it so desperately. (See more in Appendix 3.)

7

Books–Your Companion
to Natural Learning

Myself and every parent I have ever worked with desires to teach their children the critical values of honesty, courage, love, compassion, hard work, thoughtfulness, kindness, humility etc. Sometimes we question whether we are doing a good job at instilling these values. It is a daily undertaking that requires persistence and dedication. I believe the best tools to accomplish this, in addition to prayer are: Observation, Environments, Excursions AND stories.

Can you remember the first book you read that made you cry? For me it was *Where the Red Fern Grows*. I still remember the words,

"I buried Little Ann by the side of Old Dan. I knew that was where she wanted to be. I also buried a part of my life along with my dog."

Tears come freely when I re-read this book. The lessons of hard work, family relationships and sacrifices affected me at a young age and made me want to be better. When I read it to my children and other youth, I can tell they feel the same. There is always silence, followed by hushed sorrow, as we near the end of the story.

What about *Charlotte's Web*? Who can forget Wilbur and Charlotte and their sweet relationship?

"Why did you do all this for me?" he asked. "I don't deserve it. I've never done anything for you."

"You have been my friend," replied Charlotte. "That in itself is a tremendous thing."

Another book that brings beautiful memories is *The Lion, the Witch and the Wardrobe.* I yearn for Asland's purity and understand Peter and his struggles. I find myself feeling so grateful for forgiveness, recognizing that I desperately need it in my life. Children feel this too.

I've been blessed by books. I've read some magnificent ones and some very dreadful ones. I just finished reading *Watership Down* and I was sad to close the book as I savored the last few pages. Reading a few chapters each day had become like sharing time with an old friend. Closing the cover felt much like saying good-bye.

My personal belief when it comes to choosing books for your precious children - choose wisely! Books become companions to your children. Children need wholesome companions. From beautiful stories they will gather noble ideas, form honorable character, learn decency, receive courage, and acquire love. They will aspire to be like the heroes and heroines contained in the pages of books. Books also remind adults that we should strive to exemplify these characteristics.

Great books can guide your family through weeks and months of topics, discussions, activities, and studies in a way that textbooks never will. For every topic your family has a desire to learn about, there is a beautiful story that will open the imagination and encourage further discovery. Listen to this introduction of a phenomenal writing titled, *Book of Marvels*.

> "Dear Reader: When I was a boy in school my favorite subject was geography, and my prize possession my geography book....I loved that book because it carried me away to all the strange and romantic lands. ...The stories of such things always set me to dreaming, to yearning for the actual sight and touch of these world wonders.

> Sometimes I pretended I had a magic carpet, and without bothering about tickets and money and farewells, I'd skyrocket away to New York or to Rome, to the Grand Canyon or to China, across deserts and oceans and mountains. I often said to myself: 'I wish my father, or somebody, would take me to all these wonderful places. What good are they if you can't see them? If I ever grow up and have a son, we are going traveling together. I'll show him Gibraltar and Jerusalem, the Andes and the Alps, because I'll want my boy not only to study geography – I'd like for him to live it too.' Well I'm grown up now. But as yet I haven't any son or any daughter to go traveling with me. And so, in their places, may I take you?

> Your Friend, Richard Halliburton."

Who can read this without wanting to plan an Excursion themselves? The rest of the book is just as inspiring, as the author takes us to every corner of the world through real stories of his life adventures. Contrast these stories with a typical text book approach to geography and see how you feel when you're done.

Books should be your "go to" resource as you include Natural Learning. With books as your guide, you will not have to spend a lot of time planning activities. All you have to do is take a trip to the library and pull some books from the shelves that match up with the Observations and inspirations in your notebook.

I suggest you always take a trip to the library by yourself to begin. Alone you can focus on the many wonderful titles and find high quality books that will inspire your children. Be sure to select a good variety including nonfiction and fiction. Look through autobiographies and biographies. Check out the history section and the travel section. Bring home some recipe books, some comic books and some programming books as your children's desires dictate. Next time bring your children and let them do the same.

Sit down and look through your books together. Listen to the comments your children make. What is exciting to them? What do they ask questions about? What ideas are evolving as they search the pages? Grab your Observation Notebook and record the conversations. Books lead to questions, activities and projects. For Example, our cooperative group decided to read "My Side of the Mountain." We were fascinated and rather dumbfounded with the idea of such a young man going into the mountains on his own. We decided it must have been frightening and invigorating. He certainly learned a lot about survival. Could we ever do something like this?

Someone in our class came up with the idea of camping together for a night with the rule that we could bring only 3 things. We wanted to try to "survive" just like Sam Gribley. By three things we meant literally three things. One sleeping bag, one water bottle and perhaps one item of food OR we could give up our water bottle and bring some matches or some flint and steel OR we could bring three food items and give up our sleeping bag. Everyone had to choose for themselves.

The night of the campout came. Almost everyone had a sleeping bag and almost no one had food. Some of the boys made a makeshift fishing pole. Let's just say we didn't have a fish fry that night. Many of us tried grasshoppers for dinner. Once we got past the crunchiness, we decided they weren't too bad. Several of the kids made a lean-to for shelter and we did manage to start a fire with the flint and steel that was contributed.

There was a lack of clean water, toilet paper, s'mores, chairs, and tin foil dinners. Most of us slept without pillows, which wasn't a big deal since we didn't really sleep much at all. It was difficult, but fun. We were, however, grateful to get out of "survival mode" and back to our comfortable homes the next day.

We probably would not have come up with such an idea on our own—I might not have minded that either— but after our experience we knew how to start a fire without a match and how

not to go fishing. We had a greater appreciation for modern-day conveniences as well. *My Side of the Mountain* was our inspiration.

The books you bring home from the bookstore, the library or the thrift store will be a mainstay in providing loads of ideas, projects and fieldtrips. Some of them will simply be for fun. The really great books will teach beautiful ideas, inspire discussion, invoke emotion, and bring joy. These are the books you want to line your shelves with. These are the books you want to read from together. These are the books you want to invest in.

My grandson recently found a book about geodes. He became fascinated with their formation, their beauty and breaking them open. His mother shared his captivation with me and my imagination took off. The next time they came to visit I took him and his little brother to the local rock shop to find a geode. We also picked out a few additional rocks that were interesting to the boys.

I have a neighbor and friend who is a rock hound and has an awesome workshop at his home. It is full of rocks and tools and all kinds of mesmerizing things. After I told him what we had been doing, he invited us to bring our rocks to his shop and polish them. The boys weren't the only ones who found it addicting. We definitely had to schedule a second visit for the boys and for me! He even took us on a rock-hounding trip and showed us some locations where we were certain to find beautiful agates. Now Mason, my grandson, is learning about banded agates, petrified wood and quartz. This intriguing Environment came about because of a good book.

I absolutely have to share one final book with you. It is titled *A Child's History of the World,* and was written by V.M. Hillyer. It reads like a story and teaches of everything from the Babylonians to the Huns to Abraham Lincoln. There are so many topics to explore in every single chapter.

One year we were reading about Rome and some of the Emperors. It led to a hunt for old Roman coins. We found the coins at an online shop and then researched the best way to clean them. It was literally a treasure hunt as we scrubbed and cleaned—excitedly looking to see if our coins might contain the bust of a real Roman Emperor.

We also found resources in the form of old letters that were written by Pliny the Younger during the eruption of Mt. Vesuvius. They contained some vivid descriptions of the events from that momentous day.

A Child's History of the World will bring history to life for your children and lead them to explore any number of ideas. It makes Environments easy to set up as interests are sparked. This is true of all great books and the wonders found within their pages.

A dear friend of mine shared a brilliant idea with me several years ago. He recommended that fathers take on the role of reading out loud to their children on a regular basis. Then he took it a step further and suggested that dads acquire a small bookshelf for each of their children so they can start their own collection of favorite books. These books will be theirs to take with them as they leave home for internships, college or to begin their own family. Children generally hold these books in high esteem and will get very excited about adding to their collection.

Before I leave this topic, may I introduce you to a lovely website started by Lisa Ripperton called the Baldwin Project. You can find it at www.mainlesson.com. On their website they state:

> "The Baldwin Project seeks to make available online a comprehensive collection of resources for parents and teachers of children. Our focus, initially, is on literature for children that is in the public domain in the United States. This includes all works first published before 1923. The period from 1880 until 1922 offers a wealth of material in all categories, including: Nursery Rhymes, Fables, Folk Tales, Myths, Legends and Hero Stories, Literary Fairy Tales, Bible Stories, Nature Stories, Biography, History, Fiction, Poetry, Storytelling, Games, and Craft Activities.
>
> Lisa states: "I maintain that we need to start... inculcating a love of literature in youngsters long before they reach their teenage years. This Web Site is my answer. Thanks for your support."

Thanks to Lisa for her hours of loving dedication to this project. I have been using it for years, and it is a treasure! As you take time to peruse this website you will be thrilled to find resources on hundreds of topics. The best part is that all of the books are high quality books with strong values infused in each story.

For additional suggestions of my favorite books and resources, please see Appendix 1.

8

Cheers and a Challenge

When someone reads a book such as this, it's easy to imagine that the author's life is practically perfect—that if we simply incorporate the principles of their book, our lives will be magically transformed and we will experience a life of bliss. Not true! No author or neighbor or psychiatrist or television star has a life of bliss—except in our own imaginations. Though it may sound delightful, it would be highly detrimental to our growth. Each day brings the opportunity to learn, to find happiness, to overcome challenges, to gain experience, to love and to serve. Indeed it is an opportunity to figure things out for ourselves and to gain the wisdom that comes from doing so.

My perspective is simply a little different than yours since I am at the end of my homeschooling journey. Because of my perspective I have a great desire to cheer you on and give encouragement for you to stay on the path. Looking back I see that it was an exciting, exhausting and memorable path. Granted some days it looked more like a really narrow trail, going uphill, with a cliff on both sides, and the possibility of thunderstorms, but only occasionally. I'm even a little envious of the adventures ahead of you. For me they are now sweet memories and I treasure them all!

I guarantee you are going to struggle, get frustrated and question yourself. That's when you go back to your family's foundational principles and let them soak in again. Afterward pick yourself up, reward yourself with your favorite treat (Heaven knows you deserve it) and keep moving. **I promise you there will be many beautiful days sprinkled along your way. Focus on those.**

Before writing this book I spent over a year with two different groups of moms who were either currently homeschooling or making the decision to homeschool. I issued the challenge for them to join me in Natural Learning. At the end of our time together *every single mother* had incorporated the ideas of Natural Learning. They also gained lasting friendships, even starting their own cooperative groups where they continue to love and support one another.

The Natural Learning process was easier for some parents than for others, but they each had their "lightbulb" moments. Some started by dipping their toe in the water while others dove in headfirst. They began with lots of questions and ended as mentors themselves. Their stories are compelling and beautiful.

Now I enthusiastically issue you the same challenge—to take on Natural Learning! Give it a try for the next several months. You have nothing to lose and much to gain.

Join our community at aspenschooling.com where I look forward to hearing *your* story. Utilize the tools of Observation, Environments and Excursions—along with the beautiful resource of books. Determine your family's foundational principles and don't look back! Believe in yourself. Make powerful decisions that will change the future of your family. Take control for it's your life. Your journey will be fun, exhausting, inspiring AND at the end of the day you'll be grateful you took that brave leap forward—Naturally!

Appendix 1

A Few of Val's Favorite Books and Resources

Fairyland of Science by Arabella Buckley

Where the Red Fern Grows by Wilson Rawls

Book of Marvels by Richard Halliburton

My Side of the Mountain by Jean Craighead George

American Book of Golden Deeds by James Baldwin

Scriptures

Hurlburt's Story of the Bible

Chicka Chicka Boom Boom by Bill Martin

The Little Mouse, The Red Ripe Strawberry and the Big Hungry Bear by Don Wood

Science in Your own Backyard by Elizabeth K. Cooper

The Storybook of Science by Jean Henri Fabre

The Secret of Everyday Things by Jean Henri Fabre

Watership Down by Richard Adams

The Country Diary of an Edwardian Lady

Fairy Houses by Tracy Kane

The Secret Garden by Francis Hodgson Burnett

Charlotte's Web by E.B. White

Heidi by Johanna Spyri

Swiss Family Robinson by Johann David Wyss

Tales from Shakespeare by Charles and Mary Lamb

Handbook of Nature Study by Anna Botsford Comstock

Charlotte Mason Original Home schooling Series

A Child's History of the World by VM Hillyer

A Child's Geography of the World by VM Hillyer

The Nursery Book of Bible Stories by Amy Steedman

The Golden Windows by Laura E. Richards

Little Women by Louisa May Alcott

Little Men by Louisa May Alcott

Eight Cousins by Louisa May Alcott

Nursery Rhymes

Fairytales

The Baldwin Project @ www.mainlesson.com

An Everyday Story @ www.aneverydaystory.com

Steve Spangler Science @ www.stevespanglerscience.com

A fun watercolor class for beginners:

www.youtube.com/watch?v=yUid250kRe0

Put all those "pretty rocks" to use:

www.prudentpennypincher.com/100-best-painted-rocks/

Noodle Obstacle Course:

https://www.youtube.com/watch?v=bbWNBcxVMdA

All kinds of Music - From epic orchestrations to Walt Disney to Songs of America to hymns to Broadway musicals. Music makes us feel happy, motivated, encouraged and inspired. Use it every day!

https://www.youtube.com/watch?v=5DiMoehAeOU

https://www.youtube.com/watch?v=QNwsV8w4d3M

When you don't know where to begin, choose something below and just get started!

Measuring, camping, earning, acting, singing, drawing, hypothesizing, graphing, knitting, estimating, sporting, hiking, digging, jumping, laughing, biking, building, imagining, dreaming, goal setting, shopping, dressing up, reading, pretending, smelling, dancing, floating, painting, journaling, running, surveying, eating, talking, mowing, cleaning, vacationing, discussing, serving, sharing, creating, engineering, cutting, tracing, praying, counting, shivering, climbing, blogging, fishing, babysitting, welding, smiling, roller-skating, swinging, reminiscing, baking, weighing, decorating, hoping, practicing, performing, winning, wishing, sledding, wondering, sweating, sledding, supporting, celebrating, researching, questioning, asking, struggling, overcoming, loving, listening, understanding, driving, weeding, flying, sailing, swimming, programming, writing, watching, pondering, giggling...

Appendix 2

The full list of 59 most important life skills according to British parents - in order of importance.

1. Always say please and thank you

2. Respect your elders

3. Show good table manners

4. Always tell the truth

5. Don't talk to strangers

6. Brush your teeth properly twice a day

7. Treat others with kindness

8. Be confident

9. Be helpful

10. Admit when you're wrong

11. Work hard at school

12. Know when to say 'No'

13. Save money and spend it wisely

14. Be independent

15. Learn how to swim

16. Appreciate wildlife / animals

17. Show compassion

18. Accept defeat with grace

19. Deal with rejection and disappointment

20. Comfort others

21. Have a loving relationship

22. Don't walk home alone at night

23. Get along with people you may not like that much

24. Always look on the bright side

25. Distinguish needs from wants

26. Support yourself financially

27. How to add, subtract, multiply and divide

28. Look someone in the eye when talking to them

29. How to tie a shoelace

30. Eat your greens

31. How to ride a bike

32. How to write a thank you letter

33. Tell the time on a clock with hands

34. How to make your bed

35. Always accept a challenge

36. How to deal with tragedy

37. How to resolve a dilemma

38. How to negotiate

39. To always clear your plate after dinner

40. Read before you go to bed because it's good for you

41. How to drive a car

42. How to throw a ball

43. Don't get involved in unnecessary dramas

44. Watch TV and play video games in moderation

45. How to read a traditional map

46. How to dress for an occasion

47. How to bake a cake

48. How to give a firm handshake

49. How to tie a tie

50. How to write an essay

51. How to wrap a present

52. How to change a flat tire

53. How to fly a kite

54. How to start a fire

55. How to pitch a tent

56. How to dive into a swimming pool

57. How to do a kart-wheel

58. How to use chopsticks

59. How to open a champagne bottle

This survey was commissioned by Chessington World of Adventures Resort with Psychologist Donna Dawson participating and was published at https://www.express.co.uk/

Appendix 3

Family to Family Humanitarian Expeditions (FFHE) is a non-profit 501(c)3 corporation incorporated in 2002. FFHE has been involved in humanitarian service in México for sixteen years and has directed thousands of volunteers to assist in the goal of teaching self-reliance to individuals and families. They are currently serving at four of eleven Albergue (shelters) in the state of Queretaro, Mexico. Find them at www.ffhe.info.

I encourage each of you to consider how you can get involved with the children of Mexico, or something similar. It will bless your lives beyond measure. It has certainly blessed mine.
Val

A portion of all book royalties will be donated to *Family to Family Humanitarian Expeditions.*

Valerie Butler established *Aspen Academy of Learning* in 2002 where she has directed and taught for the past 16 years. She developed curriculum, had oversight of teacher trainings, sat on the Board of Directors and nurtured many children while there. Prior to this she home-schooled four of her own children where she learned important lessons that would help her in establishing a private school. Her own curiosity and sense of adventure developed right along with that of her children and students.

She has the privilege of being a wife, and the mother of five beautiful children. With her family and students of Aspen Academy she traveled to Mexico on four occasions to give humanitarian service. She has taken students to Washington DC, Oregon, Europe and Asia with the hope that they might better understand that learning comes through experiencing and doing.

She is an advisor and mentor to homeschooling mothers and through aspenschooling.com she shares her experiences and continuing ideas.